CUDDLY COMPANION DOGS

Written by Annabel Griffin

Illustrated by Marina Halak

First published in 2024 by Hungry Tomato Ltd
F15, Old Bakery Studios, Blewetts Wharf, Malpas Road, Truro, Cornwall,
TR1 1QH, UK.

A CIP catalog record for this book is available from the British Library.

ISBN 9781916598072

Manufactured in the USA

Discover more at
www.hungrytomato.com

CONTENTS

Words in **BOLD** can be found in the glossary.

THE WORLD OF DOGS

Get ready to explore the wonderful world of cuddly companions! From the tiny toy dogs to the amazing therapy dogs, there are so many different types of lovable dogs to discover.

WHERE DO DOGS COME FROM?

Believe it or not, all dogs are **descendants** of ancient wolves. The details of how and when wolves became dogs are still quite foggy, but it likely started when humans began to **domesticate** and train wolves, at least 14,000 years ago. Today, dogs can be found all over the world.

WHAT IS A CROSSBREED?

A **crossbreed** is a dog whose parents are from two or more different breeds. Some crosses are well-loved, as they can combine the best bits from their parent breeds. Crossbreeds and mongrels are also often less likely to have health problems than **purebreds**. You can find some popular crossbreeds on pages 22-23.

WHAT IS A BREED?

A breed is a particular group of dogs that all share the same (or very similar) appearance and **characteristics**, making them easy to identify. There are hundreds of different breeds, and they can vary wildly in size, shape, hairiness, and personality.

Not all dogs belong to a specific breed. Some dogs, known as mutts or mongrels, are a mixture of lots of different breeds. They can make fantastic pets, and can often be found looking for a loving home at rescue or **rehoming shelters.**

GETTING A DOG?

Maybe you already have a dog in your family, or maybe you'd like to in the future. Owning a dog can be fun and rewarding, but it's also a big responsibility. Some dogs need a lot of space, time and attention. Before buying or **adopting** a dog, you should always carefully research their breed and think about whether you are able to give them everything they need to be happy.

BREED GROUPS

Dog breeds are often arranged into seven different groups, that are loosely based on the jobs that they were originally bred to do.

SPORTING GROUP

Also known as gundogs, these dogs were originally bred to help hunters retrieve birds.

NON-SPORTING GROUP

This is the group for dogs that don't fit into any of the other groups, so they are quite a mixed bunch!

TERRIER GROUP

This group were originally bred to hunt burrowing animals, such as rats, rabbits, foxes, and badgers. Most of them have "terrier" as part of their name.

WORKING GROUP

Dogs in this group were originally bred to perform practical tasks, such as pulling sleds and carts. They were also often used as watchdogs. They are usually large dogs.

SIGHTHOUNDS

These dogs are usually long, lean and very fast.

SCENT HOUNDS

These dogs have droopy ears and powerful noses.

HOUND GROUP

Hounds were bred for their sense of smell or sight, and were usually used for hunting. They can be split into two sub-groups: sighthounds and scent hounds.

HERDING GROUP

This group includes dogs that were bred to work on farms; herding and guarding livestock, such as sheep and cows.

TOY GROUP

Tiny breeds that are small enough to sit in your lap fall into this group. They are bred mostly as pets and companions.

CUDDLY COMPANIONS

It is often said that dogs are "mankind's best friend". They can be loving, loyal and funny companions. Some dogs are even able to provide emotional and physical support to people who need them. From fluffy little lapdogs to supportive **service dogs**, the dogs in this book all make fantastic human companions.

Pug

These popular pups have a long history as **lapdogs**. They were the valued companions of ancient Chinese emperors, and became popular among wealthy Europeans, from the 16th century. Their squished faces often lead to difficulty breathing, and other health problems.

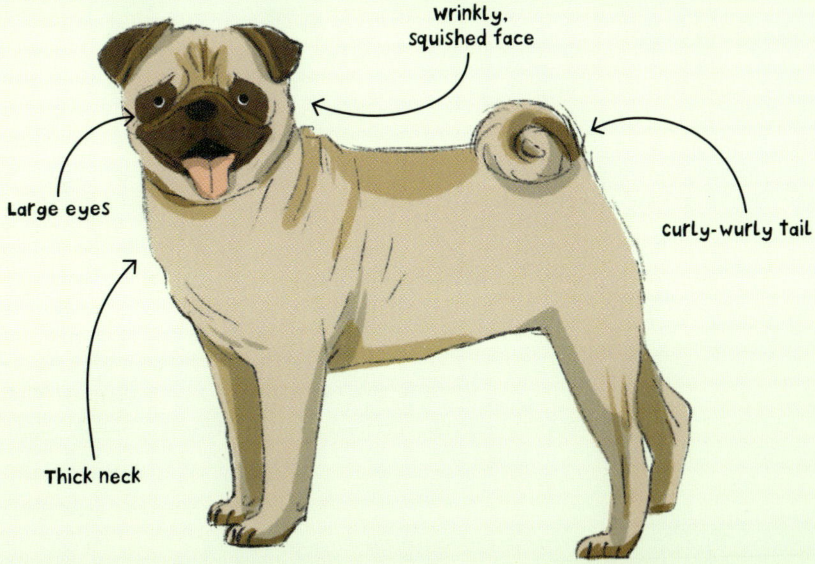

ORIGIN: China

COAT: Short, smooth

PERSONALITY: Loving and mischievous

INTELLIGENCE	3/5 paws
ENERGY LEVEL	3/5 paws
TRAINABILITY	4/5 paws

Papillon

This tiny breed can be easily identified by its large, feathery ears. Papillons appear on the laps of royalty in many old European paintings. They are affectionate dogs who love to play.

ORIGIN: France/Belgium

COAT: Medium-length, silky

PERSONALITY: Smart and friendly

INTELLIGENCE	●●●●●
ENERGY LEVEL	●●●●○
TRAINABILITY	●●●●●

Boston Terrier

This smart-looking little dog is nicknamed "the American Gentleman". They make good pets for people who live in towns and cities. They are playful and love people.

ORIGIN: USA

COAT: Short, smooth

PERSONALITY: Funny and outgoing

INTELLIGENCE	●●●○○
ENERGY LEVEL	●●●●○
TRAINABILITY	●●●●○

Brussels Griffon (Griffon Bruxellois)

This unusual toy breed (see page 7) has a big personality for its size! They are playful and easy to train. They love to be part of the family and can get lonely when left on their own for too long.

ORIGIN: Belgium

COAT: Medium-length, **wiry**

PERSONALITY: Loyal and playful

INTELLIGENCE	3 of 5 paws
ENERGY LEVEL	3 of 5 paws
TRAINABILITY	4 of 5 paws

Cavalier King Charles Spaniel

These dogs are named after King Charles II of England, who kept similar dogs. Unlike most other breeds of spaniel, who were originally bred to work, these dogs have always been kept purely for companionship.

ORIGIN: United Kingdom

COAT: Medium-length, wavy, silky

PERSONALITY: Gentle and affectionate

INTELLIGENCE	3 of 5 paws
ENERGY LEVEL	3 of 5 paws
TRAINABILITY	4 of 5 paws

French Bulldog

This mini bulldog breed is a popular pet. They are particularly good for people who live in small apartments, as they don't need a lot of outdoor exercise. They also make handy watchdogs, as they are always alert.

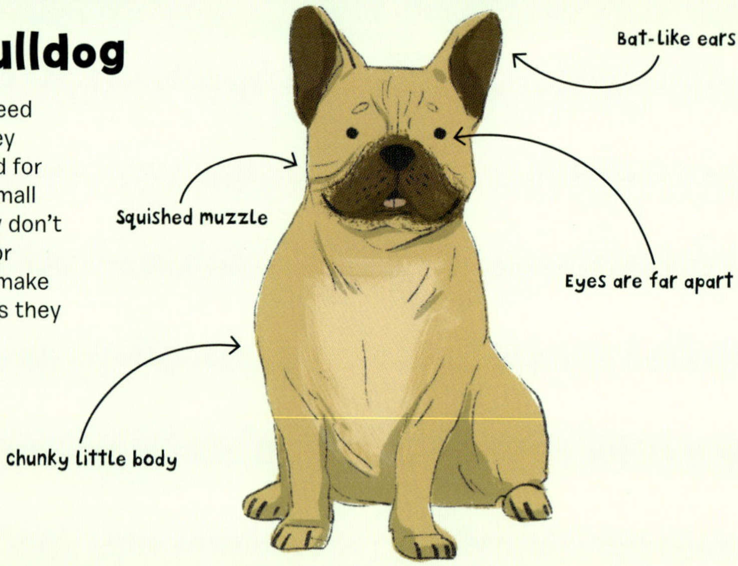

ORIGIN: France

COAT: Short, smooth

PERSONALITY: Goofy and charming

INTELLIGENCE	●●●○○
ENERGY LEVEL	●●●○○
TRAINABILITY	●●●●○

Shih Tzu

The Mandarin name "Shih Tzu" translates to "little lion" in English. Their long, fluffy coats require a lot of grooming, but they make cuddly and playful pets.

ORIGIN: China/Tibet

COAT: Long, thick

PERSONALITY: Playful and affectionate

INTELLIGENCE	●●○○○
ENERGY LEVEL	●●●○○
TRAINABILITY	●●●●○

Bolognese

These scruffy little dogs are real couch potatoes that don't require a lot of exercise. They love being with people and don't like to be left alone for long.

ORIGIN: Italy

COAT: Long, wavy

PERSONALITY: Calm and easy-going

	Rating (paws out of 5)
INTELLIGENCE	4
ENERGY LEVEL	1
TRAINABILITY	5

Japanese Chin

Despite their name, these dogs are thought to have first originated in China. They are often described as cat-like dogs, and make excellent lap-warmers!

ORIGIN: China

COAT: Medium-length, silky

PERSONALITY: Gentle and loving

	Rating (paws out of 5)
INTELLIGENCE	3
ENERGY LEVEL	2
TRAINABILITY	3

Toy Poodle

The smallest of four different sizes of the popular poodle, reaching a maximum of 10 inches (25cm) tall. They may be tiny, but they are just as smart and athletic as their larger brothers and sisters.

ORIGIN: Germany

COAT: Long, curly

PERSONALITY: Smart and confident

INTELLIGENCE	●	●	●	●	●
ENERGY LEVEL	●	●	●	●	○
TRAINABILITY	●	●	●	●	●

Miniature Pinscher

Also known as "Min Pins", these dogs are a mini breed of pinscher that look similar to the larger German pinscher and Dobermann. They were originally used as farmyard rat-hunters.

ORIGIN: Germany

COAT: Short, smooth

PERSONALITY: Fearless and outgoing

INTELLIGENCE	●	●	●	●	○
ENERGY LEVEL	●	●	●	●	●
TRAINABILITY	●	●	●	○	○

Alaskan Klee Kai

This miniature husky-type dog comes in three sizes, with a height range between 12–17 inches (30–44cm). They look similar to the much larger Siberian husky and Alaskan malamute, but were bred as house dogs, rather than to pull sleds.

ORIGIN: USA

COAT: Medium-length, extra thick

PERSONALITY: Alert and curious

INTELLIGENCE

ENERGY LEVEL

TRAINABILITY

Shetland Sheepdog

The Shetland sheepdog, or "Sheltie", is often mistaken for a mini rough collie, but they are actually separate breeds. They are one of the smartest dogs around and are incredibly loving, but they need lots of exercise and attention.

ORIGIN: United Kingdom

COAT: Long, very thick

PERSONALITY: Loyal and sensitive

INTELLIGENCE

ENERGY LEVEL

TRAINABILITY

HEROIC HELPERS

Service or assistance dogs are trained to help people with disabilities. This includes guide dogs for the blind and visually impaired, hearing dogs to assist deaf and hard of hearing people, mobility service dogs to help people with physical disabilities, and medical response dogs to help people manage medical conditions.

A service dog's duties can include helping people move around, completing household tasks, providing medical assistance, and offering emotional support and company. Lots of different breeds are used as service dogs, but some are particularly popular.

Labrador Retriever

Labs have long been the most popular dog in many countries around the world. They are loving, highly intelligent, steady, and reliable. These are all great qualities for guide dogs for the blind, and for other service and assistance work.

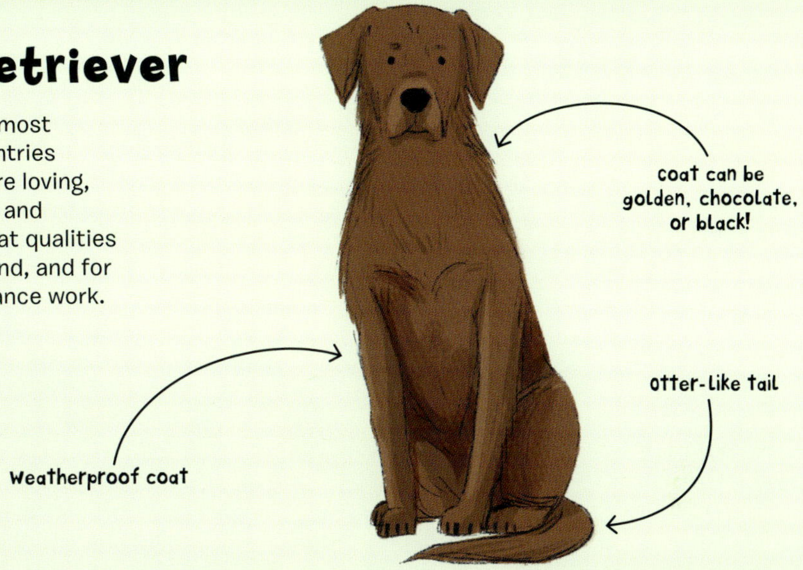

ORIGIN: Canada

COAT: Short, smooth

PERSONALITY: Lovable and loyal

INTELLIGENCE

ENERGY LEVEL

TRAINABILITY

Golden Retriever

Another very popular breed, as both family pets and for service work. Golden retrievers are big people-pleasers which makes them affectionate family pets and also smart working dogs.

ORIGIN: United Kingdom

COAT: Medium-length, thick

PERSONALITY: Gentle and trustworthy

INTELLIGENCE

ENERGY LEVEL

TRAINABILITY

Irish Setter

Often known simply as "red setters" because of their distinctive auburn coat. Their sweet, affectionate, and sociable personalities have made them popular as **therapy dogs**, to be taken into schools, hospitals, and nursing homes.

ORIGIN: Ireland

COAT: Medium-length, silky

PERSONALITY: Lovable and loyal

INTELLIGENCE	●●●●○
ENERGY LEVEL	●●●●●
TRAINABILITY	●●●●○

Pomeranian

Service dogs don't have to be big! Aside from being adorable balls of fluff, Pomeranians are highly intelligent and loving. They make great emotional support dogs, medical response dogs, and can also assist people who have difficulties hearing or have no hearing at all.

ORIGIN: Germany

COAT: Long, very thick

PERSONALITY: Friendly and smart

INTELLIGENCE	●●●●●
ENERGY LEVEL	●●●○○
TRAINABILITY	●●●○○

Shiba Inu

This ancient breed has been much loved in its homeland of Japan for centuries, and has recently been gaining popularity across the rest of the world.

ORIGIN: Japan

COAT: Short, thick

PERSONALITY: Bold and independant

INTELLIGENCE	3/5
ENERGY LEVEL	3/5
TRAINABILITY	2/5

English Cocker Spaniel

One of the most popular spaniel breeds, English cocker spaniels are energetic, alert, and loyal. They can make fun and affectionate pets for active families.

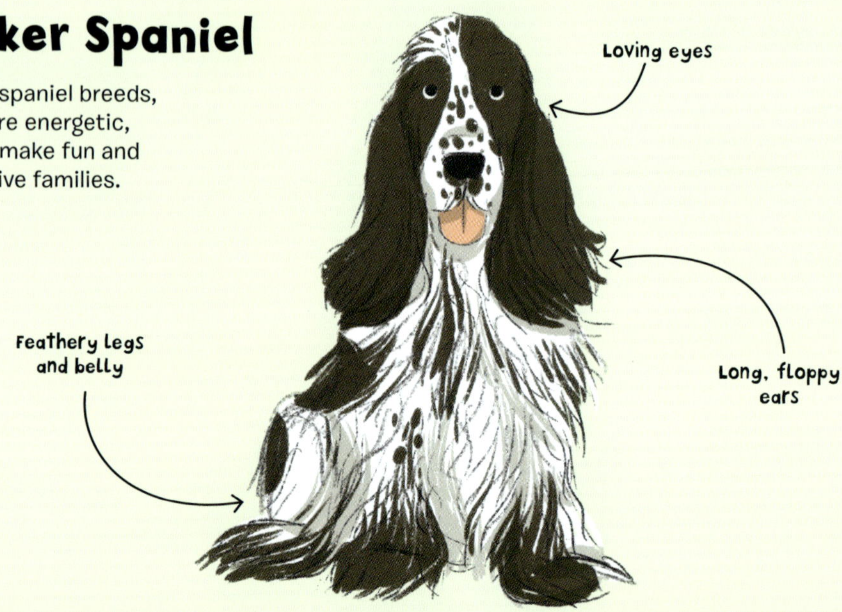

ORIGIN: United Kingdom

COAT: Medium-length/long, wavy

PERSONALITY: Friendly and outgoing

INTELLIGENCE	5/5
ENERGY LEVEL	4/5
TRAINABILITY	4/5

Staffordshire Bull Terrier

"Staffies" often have a bad **reputation** because of their history as fighting dogs, but they are actually some of the sweetest, most affectionate dogs you will ever meet!

ORIGIN: United Kingdom

COAT: Short, smooth

PERSONALITY: Brave and loyal

INTELLIGENCE	●●●○○
ENERGY LEVEL	●●●●○
TRAINABILITY	●●●●●

Shar-Pei

This unusual-looking breed is thought to have developed from ancient Chinese guard dogs. They came near to **extinction** in the 1970s, but are now a popular breed across the world. Unfortunately, irresponsible breeding for a more wrinkled look has increased their risk of health problems.

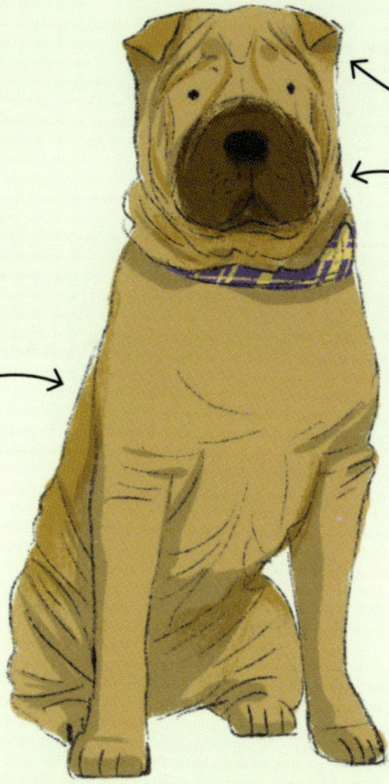

ORIGIN: China

COAT: Short, smooth

PERSONALITY: Lovable and loyal

INTELLIGENCE	●●●○○
ENERGY LEVEL	●●●○○
TRAINABILITY	●●●○○

Labradoodle

Labradoodles are a cross between a Labrador retriever (page 17) and a poodle. They have become incredibly popular family dogs. They are smart, energetic, and people-loving.

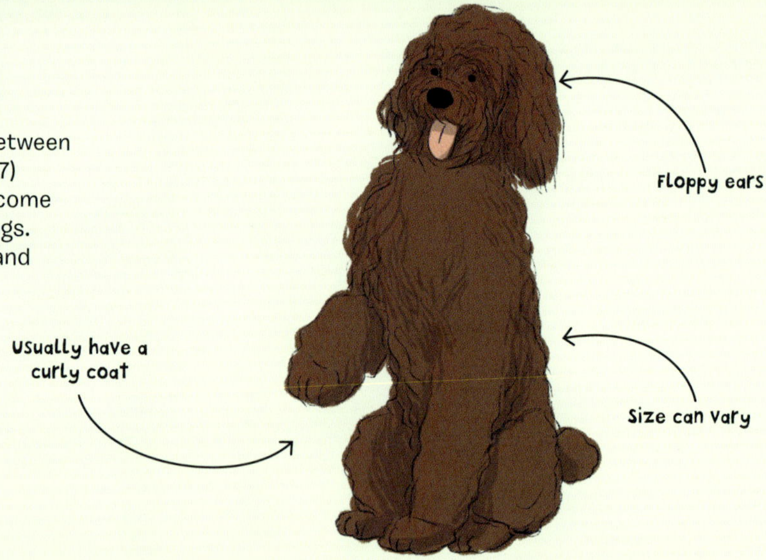

ORIGIN: Australia

COAT: Medium-length, curly

PERSONALITY: Playful and friendly

Lurcher

Lurchers are a cross between a sighthound (see page 7), such as a greyhound or whippet, and a terrier or herding dog. They are usually gentle and quiet dogs who love to run, but spend lots of their time relaxing and snoozing, too.

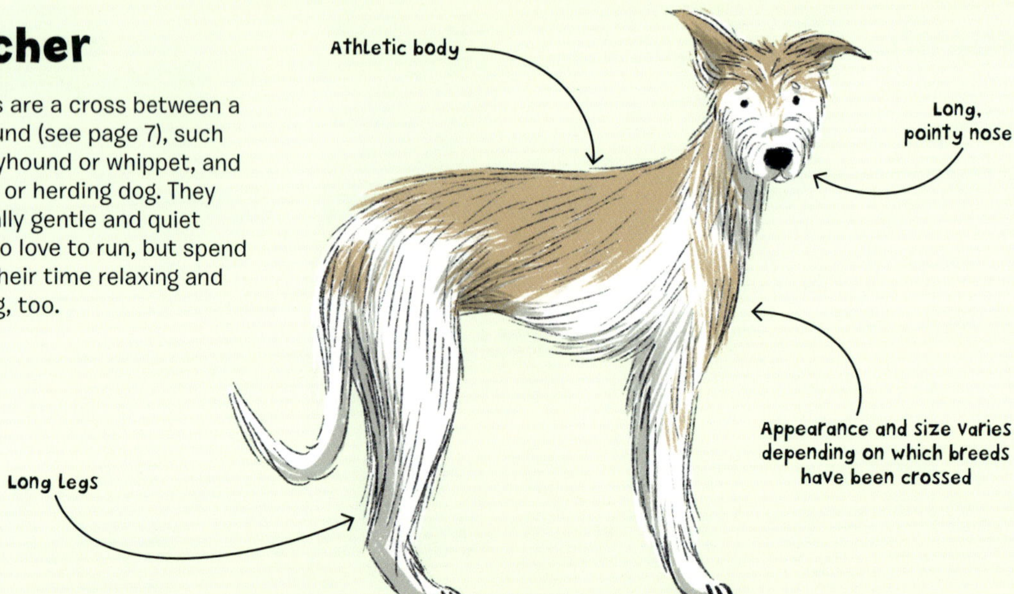

ORIGIN: United Kingdom

COAT: Short, smooth or wiry

PERSONALITY: Peaceful and loving

Puggle

A puggle is a cross between a pug (page 9) and a beagle. They are taller and more energetic than a pug, and are less likely to have health issues.

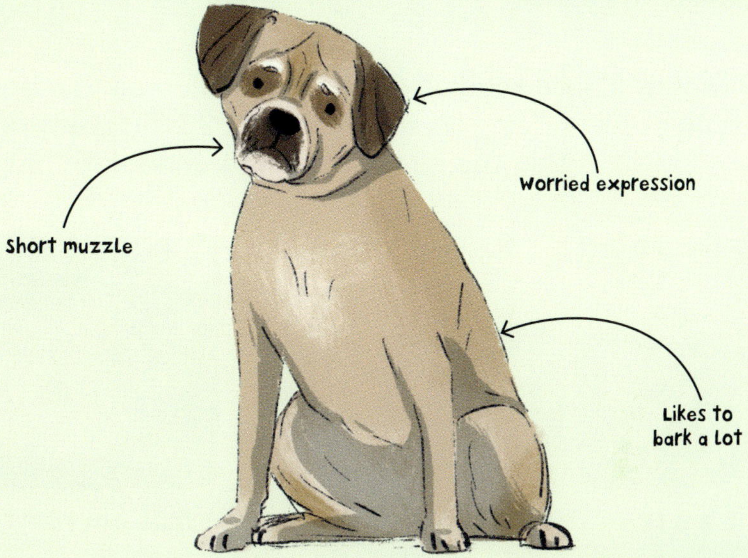

ORIGIN: USA	**INTELLIGENCE** 3/5
COAT: Short, smooth	**ENERGY LEVEL** 3/5
PERSONALITY: Bouncy and outgoing	**TRAINABILITY** 3/5

Cavachon

This cute little pup is a cross between a Cavalier King Charles spaniel (page 11) and a bichon frisé. They can make fun-loving, loyal companions.

ORIGIN: USA	**INTELLIGENCE** 3/5
COAT: Medium-length, wavy or curly	**ENERGY LEVEL** 4/5
PERSONALITY: Cuddly and playful	**TRAINABILITY** 5/5

WHAT'S THAT DOG?

Now you have read all about cuddly companion dogs, how good are you at identifying them? There are 25 different dogs to figure out. Use the information in the book to help you.

What am I?
A. Shiba Inu
B. Lurcher
C. Labradoodle

What am I?
A. Cavachon
B. Alaskan Klee Kai
C. Shar Pei

What am I?
A. Puggle
B. Papillon
C. Shih Tzu

What am I?
A. Labrador Retriever
B. Irish Setter
C. Shiba Inu

What am I?
A. Boston Terrier
B. Shetland Sheepdog
C. Irish Setter

What am I?
A. Cavachon
B. Pug
C. Bolognese

What am I?
A. Japanese Chin
B. Shar Pei
C. Miniature Pinscher

What am I?
A. Toy Poodle
B. Pomeranian
C. Japanese Chin

What am I?
A. Cavalier King Charles Spaniel
B. Bolognese
C. Staffordshire Bull Terrier

What am I?
A. English Cocker Spaniel
B. Golden Retriever
C. Boston Terrier

What am I?
A. Pug
B. Brussels Griffon
C. Papillon

What am I?
A. Staffordshire Bull Terrier
B. Shar Pei
C. Miniature Pinscher

13

What am I?
A. Shiba Inu
B. Puggle
C. Irish Setter

Answers can be found on page 32.

14

What am I?
A. Japanese Chin
B. Boston Terrier
C. Lurcher

15

What am I?
A. Toy Poodle
B. Cavachon
C. English Cocker Spaniel

16

What am I?
A. Alaskan Klee Kai
B. French Bulldog
C. Golden Retriever

17

What am I?
A. Pomeranian
B. Staffordshire Bull Terrier
C. Labradoodle

18

What am I?
A. Shih Tzu
B. Labradoodle
C. French Bulldog

19

What am I?
A. Bolognese
B. Labrador Retriever
C. Pomeranian

20

What am I?
A. Miniature Pinscher
B. Papillon
C. Brussels Griffon

21

What am I?
A. Puggle
B. Shar Pei
C. Golden Retriever

22

What am I?
A. French Bulldog
B. Toy Poodle
C. Shetland Sheepdog

23

What am I?
A. Golden Retriever
B. Pug
C. Cavalier King Charles Spaniel

24

What am I?
A. Lurcher
B. English Cocker Spaniel
C. Shetland Sheepdog

25

What am I?
A. Shih Tzu
B. Brussels Griffon
C. Alaskan Klee Kai

SPOT THE DOG

There are so many brilliant dogs in the world. You can see them everywhere you go: in towns, parks, and sometimes even at the beach! See which of these are the most popular dogs where you live, make a note of them in a journal if you do spot them.

Brussels Griffon

Shiba Inu

Shar-Pei

French Bulldog

Alaskan Klee Kai

Pomeranian

Which dogs do you think will be the most and least common in your area? Write your guesses in a journal and check if you were right. You may be suprised how many you spot, now that you know your breeds!

Pug

Toy Poodle

Staffordshire Bull Terrier

Shih Tzu

English Cocker Spaniel

Golden Retriever

Cavachon

Labradoodle

Puggle

Lurcher

Labrador Retriever

Shetland Sheepdog

CARING FOR YOUR PUP

Owning a dog can be fun and rewarding, but it's also a big responsibility. There are lots of things to think about when looking after your four-legged friend.

Grooming

Just like people, dogs need to have their hair (fur), nails, and teeth looked after regularly. You can do basic grooming at home and take your pup to a professional groomer when they need a haircut!

Brush your pup's coat every day to stop it from tangling.

Regular baths are advised, and after a muddy walk... essential!

Dogs need their teeth cleaned too! Clean them with dog-safe toothpaste or a special chew toy.

Dogs that don't walk on hard surfaces need to have their nails clipped.

Exercise

All dogs need daily exercise. Whether you're walking around your neighborhood or playing in the dog park, your dog will love getting out and exercising. It's fun and keeps them healthy!

Some dogs, like Shetland Sheepdogs, have lots of energy and need 1-2 long walks a day.

Other dogs, like Bologneses, only need one short walk a day.

Health

It's important to make sure your dog is healthy, so pay attention if they start behaving differently to normal. Signs of illness could include:

- Limping or holding a paw off the ground
- Heavy panting for no reason
- Change to eating or drinking habits

Speak to an adult if you think something's wrong, they can take the pup to a **vet.** Vets can also provide the de-worming and flea medicines dogs need regularly to stay healthy.

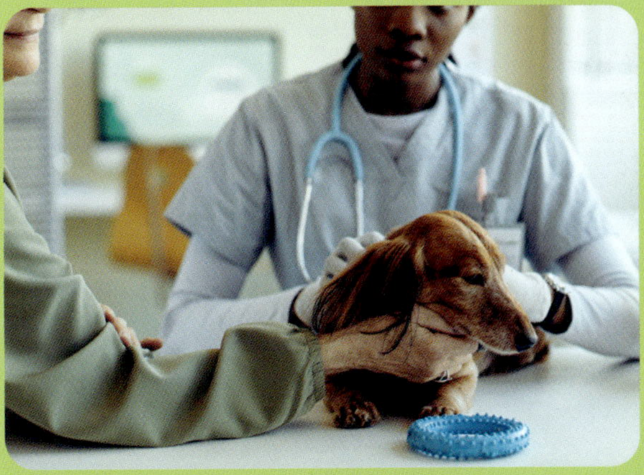

Diet

There are lots of options for dog food, including dry biscuits and tinned food. The amount your dog needs to eat every day depends on their age, size and breed. Giving them the right amount is important for keeping them healthy and happy.

Be careful if you use treats for training, you don't want to overfeed your pup!

GLOSSARY

Adopting – Legally taking on the animal as your own, receiving all responsibility.

Characteristics – a feature or quality of a person, place, or thing.

Crossbreeding (crossbreeds) – when two dogs of different breeds have puppies.

Descendants – people or animals that are related to an individual or group who lived in the past. For example, you are a descendant of your parents and grandparents.

Domesticate – to be tamed or trained to live or work with humans.

Extinction – the dying out of a species.

Lapdogs – dogs that are small enough to sit on someone's lap and make friendly companions.

Purebreds – dogs belonging to a specific breed, not a crossbreed or mongrel.

Rehoming shelter – a place where dogs (or other animals) who were lost, stray, or given up by their owners, are looked after until they can be adopted into a new home.

Reputation – A general opinion based on beliefs about a certain thing or person.

Service dog (or assistance dog) – a dog that has been trained to assist a person with a disability. Examples of service dogs include guide dogs, hearing dogs, medical response dogs, and autism service dogs.

Therapy dog – dogs that are trained to provide comfort and support to people. Unlike service dogs (see above) who only assist one person, therapy dogs help multiple individuals, or groups of people. They often work in hospitals, schools, or nursing and retirement homes.

Vet - a vet, or veterinarian, is an animal doctor. They help take care of animals when they are sick or hurt.

Wiry – a type of dog coat that is rough, thick, and bristly.

INDEX

WHAT'S THAT DOG ANSWERS

1 - B. Lurcher
2 - A. Cavachon
3 - C. Shih Tzu
4 - A. Labrador Retriever
5 - C. Irish Setter
6 - C. Bolognese
7 - B. Shar-Pei
8 - C. Japanese Chin
9 - A. Cavalier King Charles Spaniel
10 - A. English Cocker Spaniel
11 - B. Brussels Griffon
12 - C. Miniature Pinscher
13 - A. Shiba Inu
14 - B. Boston Terrier
15 - A. Toy Poodle
16 - C. Golden Retriever
17 - B. Staffordshire Bull Terrier
18 - B. Labradoodle
19 - C. Pomeranian
20 - B. Papillon
21 - A. Puggle
22 - A. French Bulldog
23 - B. Pug
24 - C. Shetland Sheepdog
25 - C. Alaskan Klee Kai

ABOUT THE AUTHOR

Annabel is a writer and artist based in London, UK. Having worked as a bookseller for many years, she now writes children's books focusing on animals and the natural world. Her recent titles include *What Can I See in the Wild?*, *Seasons* and *The Spectacular Lives of Sharks*.

ABOUT THE ILLUSTRATOR

Marina is a talented illustrator of children's books from Ukraine. Her stunning illustrations are inspired by her own childhood, children, nature, magical moments and fairytales.

Picture Credits:
(abbreviations: t=top, b=bottom, m=middle, l=left, r=right)

220 selfmade studio 25bm, 27tl; Anna Maloverjan 25mr; BIGANDT.COM 24bl; Chaoss 24tm, 27ml; Danita Delimont 25tm, 27tm; David Raihelgauz 24m, 26tr; Dezy 25ml, 27m; Dmytro Zinkevych 28ml; DragoNika 24ml; Ezzolo 29bl; Joy Brown 24tm, 27ml; Jus-01 28br; Kasefoto 28mr; Labrador photo video 24bm, 27m; Lisjatina 25bm, 27br; Littlekidmoment 28bl; Mary swift 25bl, 25mr, 26ml, 27mr; Meirion Matthias 24tl, 27bl; Momick 25br, 26m; Monkey Business Images 29mr; Nikola Cedikova 25tr, 27tr; OleysaNickolaeva 25t, 26tm; Otsphoto 24bm, 26tl; Priadilshchikova Natalia 24mr; Rala 303 25tm, 27mr; Rebeccaashworthearle 25tl; Roman Zaiets 25ml, 26mr; Rosa Joy 24tr, 27bm; SasaStock 24m; Serova_ Ekaterina 24br.